tenebraed

HELLER LEVINSON

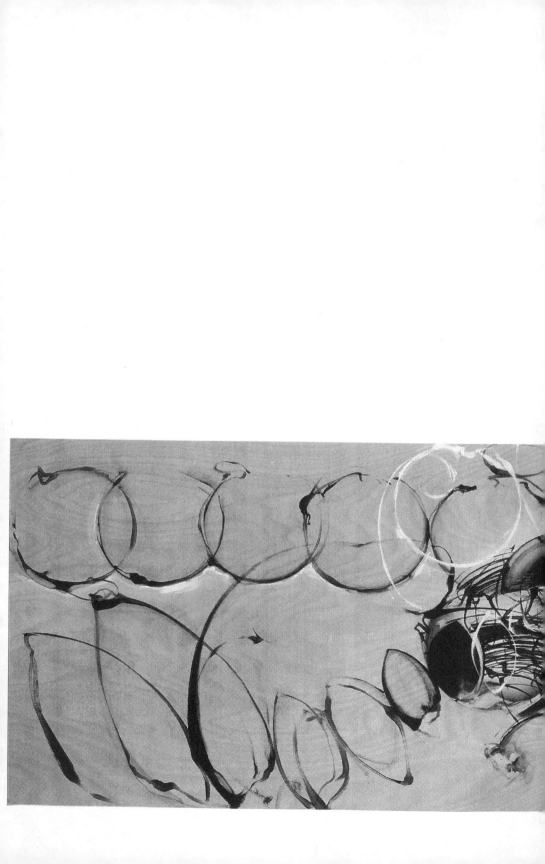

tenebraed

Black Widow Press is an imprint of Commonwealth Books, Inc., Boston, MA. Distributed to the trade by NBN (National Book Network) throughout North America, Canada, and the U.K. All Black Widow Press books are printed on acid-free paper, and glued into bindings. Black Widow Press and its logo are registered trademarks of Commonwealth Books, Inc.

Joseph S. Phillips and Susan J. Wood, Ph.D., Publishers
www.blackwidowpress.com

Art and cover design by Linda Lynch. *Oil Drawing for 2900*, detail, 2008

Text design & production: Kerrie L. Kemperman

ISBN-13: 978-0-9971725-7-7

Printed in the United States
10 9 8 7 6 5 4 3 2 1

for Michael Annis

One must forage the edges to encounter the crux.

. white tenebraes magic ≈ 46
. tenebraed to lugubrious ≈ 47
. tenebraed to singe ≈ 49
. tenebraed to step ≈ 50
. tenebraed to alternating current ≈ 51
. tenebraed to aleatory ≈ 52
. tenebraed to aleatory (first mutation) ≈ 53
. tenebraed to selection ≈ 54
. tenebraed to drought ≈ 55
. tenebraed to pact ≈ 57
. tenebraed to hunger ≈ 59
. tenebraed to dread ≈ 61
. tenebraed to mermaid ≈ 62
. tenebraed to adjacency ≈ 65
. tenebraed to old age ≈ 67
. tenebraed to drift ≈ 69
. tenebraed to Hinge Theory ≈ 71
. tenebraed to trespass ≈ 72
. tenebraed to seepage (first mutation) ≈ 73
. tenebraed to Goat Seep ≈ 74
. tenebraed to roam ≈ 77
. tenebraed to wander ≈ 78
. tenebraed to excursion ≈ 79
. tenebraed to disarray ≈ 80
. tenebraed to exhume ≈ 81
. tenebraed to finality ≈ 82
. tenebraed to loafing ≈ 83
. tenebraed to affability ≈ 84
. with tenebraed ≈ 86
. smelling tenebraed ≈ 87
. tenebraed to swarm ≈ 88

. tenebraed to a stretch mathematics ≈ 89
. tenebraed to imponderable ≈ 91
. tenebraed to petting ≈ 92
. tenebraed to attendance ≈ 94
. tenebraed to vacuity ≈ 95
. tenebraed to lamentation ≈ 96
. tenebraed to lamentation (first mutation) ≈ 97
. smelling tenebraed in the girth of lamentation (second mutation) ≈ 98
. tenebraed to perplexity ≈ 99
. tenebraed to draft ≈ 100
. tenebraed to squander ≈ 101
. tenebraed to gather ≈ 102
. tenebraed to saltatory ≈ 103
. tenebraed to tangle ≈ 104
. tenebraed to disparity ≈ 105
. tenebraed to all fours ≈ 106
. tenebraed to inclination ≈ 108
. tenebraed to vanish ≈ 109
. tenebraed to futility ≈ 110
. tenebraed to dread (first mutation) ≈ 111
. tenebraed to desuetude ≈ 113
. tenebraed to disquiet ≈ 114
. Dear Linda ≈ 116
. tenebraed to encroach ≈ 117
. tenebraed to interstice ≈ 118
. tenebraed to absence ≈ 119
. tenebraed to reverie ≈ 120
. tenebraed to parting ≈ 121

TENEBRAED CONSIDERED

In Latin, tenebrae means darkness (OED). The related adjective, "tenebrous," means dark, gloomy, or obscure (OED).

Customarily, the term "tenebrae" refers to a church service performed during the week preceding Easter. The OED defines it as:

> The name given to the office of matins and lauds of the following day, usually sung in the afternoon or evening of Wednesday, Thursday, and Friday in Holy Week, at which the candles lighted at the beginning of the service are extinguished one by one after each psalm in memory of the darkness at the time of the crucifixion. (OED)

Yet inviting darkness in the anticipation of subsequent illumination has roots preceding the Christian service. The Paleolithic artists scouring the depths of the earth to upsurge incandescent imagery are but one example.

To voluntarily enter darkness in preparation for illumination appears essential in the passage to truth: → exploring underbellies, hidden contours, liberating the undisclosed, enflaming dark hymnals,… all the while rolling, tumbling, pitching Irradiating Effulgence.

Before knowing what the word meant, I began using it in verb form. I was employing the word in "darkness" literally. I had only a hunch of something "shadowy," "obscure." When I began investigating I grew excited by the richness of the word, its "Rasa."

The possibilities of inosculating/yoking "tenebrae," "tenebrous," & "tenebrific" & germinating them into verb activity has spawned the applications seeding this enterprise. The verb "tenebraed" serves as an ignition candle to spark ruminations aspiring to enlighten the subject.[1] And when we speak of "enlighten" what do we mean? We don't mean transparency, that a particle such as "drift" will dissolve into a tidy, neatly configured notion. Often just the opposite. By pivoting off a word that is cyclically accumulative — light/dark amassing —, we destabilize the word from its platform of convenience & set it free to interrogate its own foundations. We journey. A journey encountering surprises, questions,… suggested inclinations. We come away with an Enlarged feeling for the word, one more robust, elastic,… In-Sightful.

---

[1] The "particle" in Hinge terminology.

HINGE IMPORT/EXPORT/MINE

introduced

Import

While working on "tenebraed to drift," I found myself 'drifting' to material I had applicated in other formulations. For example, 'drift' led me to consider 'seepage' which led me to explore prior 'seepage' investigations. I found that by utilizing material from these other creations I could more precisely enrich my present investigation than if compelled to rely upon language that I had never used before. In fact, just the opposite. By Importing words that had already been *placed* (positioned), that had been thought out & Earned their way, I would not only prosper the piece at hand, i.e., "tenebraed to drift," but I would Enlarge (densify) & Extend the 'Imports' by virtue of their being Freshly Re-Configured. They will have been requ(isitoned)ested to Fructify Fresh Terroir. Although of late the term "import" has taken a bad rap, imports originally enabled populations to obtain supplies & provisions that they were deficient in. Viewed prosperously, imports can be seen as Nutritional Supplements, as Life Embellishers. But it would be imprudent to draw too strict a parallel between trade importation & Hinge Importation as in Hinge the imports, the words, are *Live Organisms.*

Hinge Importation provides nutrition not only to the effulgence being served, but, just as importantly, to the words themselves. A Mutual Opulence flourishes. As the application (t' to drift') benefits from organisms that have Maturated, that have achieved Growth & Proficiency, the organisms, in turn, Bloom from their Immersions in Additional Communities, from Fresh Renascence.

Specifically: in "tenebraed to drift," the 3rd line is imported from the application "the road to lost road" (*Smelling Mary,* p.165); the 4th line also from "the road to lost road;" lines 6, 7, & 8 are from "with lines" (*Hinge Trio,* p.41); line 13, "seepage," is imported from both the application "tenebraed to seepage" & "tenebraed to goat seep"); "gloam," 18th line, heralds from "with lines;" "disarray," line 21, & line 26, "accrue," (from "tenebraed to seepage" (alternate take) are not Imports but Migratories ("seepage" is included in this section to illustrate "Migratories")[2] as they were not actively sought (solicited), they *appeared,* thus underscoring the Lawful ("each word insists on its word associates") nature of Hinge, that the word appears where it should appear. There is a precision in their Rotation similar to planetary rotation.

Export
is simply the vaulting of a word from one application to a dedicated application of its own. It transforms a word participating in an application into a particle being applicated. It 'travels' to foreign territory. The former 'participant' now becomes the Subject Scrutinized.

For example, we Exported 'trespass' from 'tenebraed to drift,' to produce 'tenebraed to trespass' (page 72). Conversely, from line 20, we Import 'border invasions' which mutates to 'border invade'.

Mining
occurs when another application is consulted to enrich the particle (application) currently being investigated. "tenebraed to Goat Seep" exemplifies a mine being tapped for its 'rich' resources.

---

2 For more on 'migratories' see *FROM STONE THIS RUNNING* (Black Widow Press), p.18.

The lexiconically Static is a Logos Abuser. It robs language of its Innate Kinetics. The lexiconic is Morbidity wrapped in the Veneer of the authoritative.

The more multiplicitous transformations a word undergoes the more it gains in Robustness, Elasticity, Dimension, & Expansion. The word becomes Invigorated, Densified, & Virile. Logos as *Ubermensch* → as "this Lightning, this Frenzy."

tenebraed to

60 x 44 inches (Linda Lynch drawing

                             oscillative sweep

                     brush-burl

                                       liturgical swirl

sough motet

swizzle-sizzle

                            sway-

                                    artfully

                         cascade

foam aurora

sessile-broth

outrig

tenebraed

**to a louche
meander**

triumphalism fails

as a calling

card

tenebraed

to a fading aristocracy. louche carom. soused soliloquy. gong. curtains. unravel. requests: for privileges. demands: for payback. fodder. borrow. usurp. pilfer. upmanship. feed. frenzy. sabotage. belly-full. belly-ache. blanche. bastion. bulldog.

: reparations; partitions; gunslingers;

fraught

fought

smatter

the finger

smithereens

accost

combust

tenure

erasure

tenebraed

to the black host

of a shorn portico

                     sigil-wraiths spore

from dune grass

                  shutter

cannonades   fustigatory shadow   maglignant rock

the Overseer

           double-bent

           hackled

           chin-scratching

turns away

tenebraed

to **an axled disposition** a susurrus fissures the brevity of
thyme
merriment inhalations overruled

you ask for qualifications the tame crab flees to the ocean & has
no place to hide

ricky ricky key–O
a'chocka' boom boom boom

true bloom sparks from interiors
landscapes void of endowment

tenebraed to a

wizened palliative the

cure-alls stammer

then

reel in disputatious

forlorn

stretching the gong of usable

pressing the lapse of a cantilevered phalanx

teeming folds

then fails

where in the

isometric

is

the host

where

the

bevel

tenebraed to **a**

polyphiloprogenitive barbarous fumarole cor

doned in the pit of viperous lucidity the history of murmurs

mounts

a rallying overviewing consummate treachery

a curse dampened by the sleight of patrimony

perfidy lampoons the gesticulate

bedlam surmounts curtailment

teamwork committed to embellishing cult uprisings reels in the

regalia of relay

with the weight of larceny the fray rattles

tenebraed

        to **a**

capsizing algorithm merchandise

spatters   rattles   decomposes.

little is lost in the

exchange.

. abbreviated cornucopias

. seldom surmises

in the circumflex of a tenebraed hedonism

jollity cheeks spangle the wind tunnels shiftless aubergines

abandon a game of trot upon which a grove of wickers gamble

it is not the sought after that goes unresolved but the vanished

now you see me now you

are but the interruption of polity glazed in mackerel

substratum of earthborn the wear worn

tenebraed

to an enameled

latency, burrowing

through hives

of collapsed vernaculars,

wracked recklessly,

the mantis of jeopardy

smooches an oblong,

trawls pearls of dismissal across confiscated skies

tenebraed

to interval

to outposts quivering from consanguinity

considering feed-back loops sideways

extremities accumulate uninteresting interest

balance wheel as bludegeon

where

in wherewithal

is

capacious

verifiability = larceny

the target is without distance

tenebraed

to acceleration

the *still* remains

tethered to an oblique omnipresent

sput ter ing

the final voice

tenebraed to a
Thorned Landscape

barbed fumarole

to atrocity sprigs spraying irradiated rampage-rain

a smolder soused in Armageddon

a solder smoldering

I walk the children down the valley for morning prayers. Our

passage is blocked by the faceless & torn.

We return the way we came.

comatose lullaby

accumulative maw

sizzling viper bellies rot the corridors, skirt perimeters, practice

venom-conservation, prepare for unilateral stabs while eviscerate

crows glob hackneyed asphalt

crimson craws the land

"Can't you see how tender I am," Themistocles responded.

astern-yank-debris models untethered adumbrations, oscillative

chelae crunch toward Bethlehem

— polyp glyphs

— churl geyser

— fetid tarantula

— dredge-cur

— the defined encases the suds of the ill-defined

griddling in the abracadabra of possum tooth, of a

cannibalistic fusion,

vexed carcasses spleen these ashgory days of diminutive sleight,

hurl reams

of necrotic dawns

in

perpetual

infarction

tenebraed to

detour

skirmish-land

the road to detour road

break   breakage   breakaway

break-up   break-off   breakfast

deter   disrupt   dissimilar   dismissal

unkempt with wayless   wayward . . .

eviscerate-path   turmoil-rendezvous

lost or circulating

"It's not in the cards," Agamemnon said.

small craft warnings

being under-way ://: over-way ://: overlay

stepping forth

                — Pre-sen-Ta-tion

forthcoming to forward

                — to-ward

arcana as kindling

                — accum-u-lation

rearward: slung recalcitrance?

pursuit with perusal

the step-forth

ensorcelled

by

linger

tenebraed to

seepage

to the vertebrae of disappearance

disparities columnize in lopsided disarray

densities convulse

calibrations formatting the well-heeled wither in inebriate

perambulation

from these halls of cirrhotic séance

loams the

first heard

a pedal's reminiscence

tenebraed

to

a worn one-inch flat hog-bristle

stroke   slosh   scrub

                              → whistle

slush-fund   funding canvas

applications contest method

method the pigment of procedure   process   getting

started

threading abyss   to negatavize the not

vacancy's leach

"I'll outcuss you at the Ceder, Joan."

Totally unprepared when she rammed my balls.

where in

license

is

licentious

the Chunking Hog slurping a continent away, did he envision his

bristles slurping across canvases on East 10 st.

where in

the

painting

is the

hog

Note: this application is dedicated to Joan Mitchell whose brush of choice was a worn one-inch flat hog-bristle.

tenebraed to

aperture

to thorned uptakes spiking antediluvian draft, a displaced sap

coats involuntary moan with pullulating grief-bricks, holdovers

from hollowed tributaries, those indented spheres trespassing

toward an advanced bellicosity, the wager sinks, the frost lost its

timing, commandeering the concealed to stall foreclosure on

estuarial rambunction an appeal aerates on the wings of earliest

reflex

tenebraed
to black

octagonal bloodbath, omnidirectional swallow,

heaving capillary burst, reformers cold outside, fringe-frost-frigid, furtive pyre-belch, tapering to a maddening allusive sponge-mollusks hurdle moribundity-boulders, the concupiscence of remote seals the landscape, . . .

"Mes faims, c'est les bout d'air noir. My hungers are the ends of black air." — Rimbaud

"Black is the darkest of colors." — Wittgenstein

"How fair is your hair, Henrietta." — Heller

errant grief pockets tribulate robotic bite tentacles abbès rock solid yet wobbly peculiar the air sustenance ://: sustain the meek backdoor landlords with piety purify purity purification is overrated it's soot black hawks twisting through velvet,
it's coming to the wardrobe with vast undercurrent ..

. . .

Black is color's barometer

alpha & omega wrapped in *p-l-u-n-g-e*

beheaded muffle

bleached murmur

"we do not have to understand black, it is the primordial ground."
— Paul Klee

in the dwindle of eternal taper baptizing sublunary flagellations

White whisk-spills in the tryst garden craters diligence dalliance

pinwheels recruitable doubts . . . .

which color more resembles Nothing, — black or white?

"Pitch was traditionally used to help caulk the seams of wooden
sailing vessels. Pitch was also used to waterproof wooden contain-
ers, and in the making of torches. Petroleum-derived pitch is black
in colour, hence the adjectival phrase, '**pitch-black**'." → mobilize
pitch

torn mourn bundle the berths brindle, (en)lighten, securitize →

ominous cumulonimbus empyreal vase-vessel rain-pour → from

dark this nutrition, this backflipping imprimatur, a thrust suddened

by the thirst for quiescence . . . .

S saw duende as burnt orange. This was at odds with Raoul who

argued that duende could only be black. The deep black of Andalusian

flamenco, of the soulful-somber-hypnotically tragic. S waged for a more

ambi(guous)(tious) translation referring to underground root systems

milling motile vitals in the dark hidden. She spoke of black as the

emancipated feminine, as the highly sexed absorbing All.

"Of absence, darkness, death: things which are not" puncture: an

ooze permit, a *letting*

letting the puncture that drools   penumbra numbing

nocturne abet , the slaughter of odds,

dissipates rule the order . . . nowhere is the fraught more severe

this strickening you speak of, Mister Hughes, does it have a name?

Speak, Black, . . . Speak

→

louche demeanor roseate cheek-chops churn bloom from incinerate
frost rectify gamboling urn plinth, →

Black: fleshy, transmundane, — *frothfull,*

feral castanet gland swell island hopper runnel blast #5 mournful
melancholic cape swaggering juju broth admissible annihilative
churly warren-breasted perfume-knolls rockabilly dearth rags
perforate opulent fringe

the sound: wolves leaf-settling

odor: a withering parentheses

vaporous whales chug the shoreline curtseying to forelegs wrack
lariats indemnify domestication

forebode ://: lode

load   loading   fully-loaded   perpetually consummate

S pondered whether black had an ideal temperature, . . . perhaps all
colors had an ideal temperature. Living things functioned best at their
ideal temperatures. Let there be a Color Congress insuring appropriate
thermostatting.

Black: infinity's gangplank

smoke   cinder   ash →   geometric meltdown

basking in hound saliva

husk exercises in an obsolete burlesque

tenebraed

to

bleed out run

rut

rutting in pools of ghost mist calibrations languish, bramble
epidermal berms with

incapacity

a waywardness
draining

tenebraed to

nothing

to the not that is not

> [Nothing: "No thing; not anything." (OED)]

a clot on surreption's baseline

cancellation's triumph

paltry bemusement

B   L   A   N   K

S couldn't get excited. about anything. it was worse than having the wind knocked out of you. it was being void of wind to wind up with.

craters crow-void in the husk of disintegrating saliva

to speak of nothing is something

absence ab*sents*

the road to nullity road

can nothing endure?

without?

out with the old ....

in

with

withIn nothing

being within out

"being & nothingness"

the ineptitude of exactitude

does nothing have color

nothing technicolor-ed

void   avoid   vitiate

trammeling the root, the ubiquity of singe, burnt orange overarches

constitutions,

stars: mournful exhibitions,

abstentia's reek

with genesis this *nam-ing*

from blot this *blight*

kilter kelter the spank of reduction → riddance

steadfast

unerring

empty

white tenebraes magic

what else can get the job done what other can rectify when the
allotment is narrow & the obsequies vague   ; overdrawn , , , there
you go leading off with a question when results only matter.
pulling strings from a hat . like .   the shape of things to come
ditto ;; , please, the whale was vast but pallid . it fought its pallor
ferociously. a thing of the past is not without scrutiny. this is a
poem about the mid-east. ask me how i know it. because i can
throw it. throwing is authentic , , it's body speak. missiles are
inauthentic though they are large on impact. ; ;   stripping down
the quilt to fiber ,. ,. the delights of enterprise have yet to be
fathomed.   could you please not speak for me , Mr. Phillips. i
know my own tongue *** a language not marred by controversy , ,
untappedmapped through soliloquy
,, ;
the shape of a reticent disjunction disqualifies me from making
sense , , , certainly my dressage scores suffer , . .
, sense being the purest form of nonsense.
, olatunji
. you are what you vision

tenebraed

to

lugubrious

lung   longe   lunge

lung-full   allocation   affectation's turntable

afford-a-bil-ity

banjogriddling headlight cacophony penalties bloat tragic tapes

reel reek streamline myrrh mired newscasters smirk calamities

could you please repeat your question, please, the aforementioned

going happily from place to place tires belch a failed prehistory

Suicide on the tracks has passengers interrogating delay

memory no longer serves but severs   ,restated, your question is

sound but terribly dated

Mrs. Hartley never wanted to be on the school board anyway but

positively thrilled when appointed chief of the town's Dread

Removal dept.

the cartography of duty

passage ://: comeuppance   → circumstance

when does the reprehensible become noteworthy

flower ladies drooping grime arrive late for backgammon

the only game in town now

lost

so

terribly lost

tenebraed to

singe

placative burn

plaintive bandit crawler

cagey outlander fierce underpin border rigger

hours in accumulative collapse

pause of the killer claw

murmurs slipper eel lips

cicatrix   susurration   callow   incise

eddy

crepitant

Sphinx on a plinth

piercings

rattle

tenebraed to

step

step up   leg up   stepping

steeped

sleek among the millstones the tread

stepping the road

                                        the inevitability of

road

                                        along the way

path finder

plot

tenebraed to

alternating current

spool moss, the stuff of bridges, where you go when the weather

defeats, — drag of laborious days . . .

disposition at odds with deposition

more cream less sugar hold the mayo sinusoidal coital wring

waggle wiggle wrung bell tower churn chump change jingle jangle

junkyard wrangle put on hold gosh it's cold coruscate habeas

corpus writ large I love you I love you too how do you do do do

dawn mantle

deer dorsal

gong meander

whistle lard

lump recalcitrant

the boulders so slowly so lowly girdling dispatch over there beyond

the sunset issue forth peddle perturb arise surmise

dribble

dawn

tenebraed to

aleatory

dice riddle

motley

woebegone   fiddle   turn of the screw

S adored the tables. Loved Monaco. Loved splendor, the intoxication of

risk, — knowing, winning all, or losing all, She, bedecked in titillating

taffeta & the finest jewelry, had Chosen.

causal malfunction

choice the annunciator

ausculated silt a pause in the prance of a Percheron

S knew how to fuck. this was all she required to feel good about herself.

the swindle was adept & took all by surprise

tenebraed to

aleatory (first mutation

hit   miss

      reper-cuss

churl chidder   clam bake

          chin chadder chatter stall

burlesque presupposes sobriety patches the uprisings never further

away than earshot early morning coition larks the underside of the

vessel garners the most barnacles

do not disturb artist awake

the revolution of independence requires a beginning

saddle sores & discrepancies

seasonal reluctance

tenebraed to

selection

        to

this not that   randomrudderscufflesortfileprehend*ap*prehend

                                   pick & choose

elicit ,   , . .

the bring-forth coils the cull

arbitrage muzzles the asylum

an upstart nation

floodlit

devout

pandering fits & follies of pedigree free choice questions melt to

tambourine moisture

to alloy

to tubes

to

a plethora of tools

tenebraed to

drought

rasp reticula   hoarse

harsh suspend

bereft

yearn pile-up ,   ,

a blink liquefies

jurisdiction another campaign for adjudication especially the

leftovers ripe with advocacy vote for lumber

without her without her without with out

numb

absentee draft

parch

without impregnates with

the close at hand

undertow menaces relinquish

drought: the taking away?

       the not enough of?

there no longer there: absence

stepping absents

here to there

step: tectonic

     reverential

     grammatical

saturation depletes with overabundance

measure, mete out , . . .

carburate

how much of

you

can I take with me

tenebraed to

pact

un-liveried   fair

        clasp

        bond

        brethren

blood-mesh

anarchical spurn

sprint-laden in combustive archaeologies the solvency of resilience

reliance   lie-upon   lay to rest

lean-in   lean-upon

solution

compound

combinatory   comfort   commode   accommodate

support   resolve

steadfast

gird   endure

word-pact/

    impact/

        impart

distribution

Other with/to Other   suffuse   transfuse

fusion

transfusion

fusion: confusion's absolution

to bond, plunge, . . . the unmediated,

call-out to Under-Taking

add-on

supplemental

graft

tenebraed to

hunger

pang   empty *pier–cing*

forsook pillage

ferocity fang

fungal creep

slurred absenteeism

>"Sentience arises from predator avoidance.
>
>> We are conscious because we might be eaten."

escape claw

hatch gambol arboreal clutch

tangle terrestrial

   how much of

   relief

   is

   gestural

culprit compromise

belabored bedlam

in the loll of boll weevil waxen stitch incremental device drive

turret cluster flavor savors cartographic demise

hitch

post peristaltic

mathematics of belly

of, → belly-Full

calculating full-Fill-Ment

belly-Wrack: earth's mantra

tenebraed to

dread

ill at ease   queasy   missteps

ramparts pocked, pillaged, squalls of blood thirst, a tear stretching

to incomplete,

terror-smolder, without latch or key, belly chopped, cognitive

dismember, upended unconditionally, final, . . . strewn_____

rattle gear rust wreck dilapidation, — hexed

….………. demise

pit storms   smother moths

tribunal roaches   noose angels

savagery   the unabated

privilege overdue, payment required

tooth-bleed   gnat gnaw   swine vomit

exit stall

                                    quicksand

                                    landslide

                                    permafrost

everywhere you turn . . . Nowhere

not even a not to constitute

the inconsolable tacked to leprous creep

tenebraed to

mermaid

to blue algae bludgeon slur

scrape of solar scrim

two-world strider slippering through wave-lap

where do you like it best?

land? sea?

Hans Peter Duerr writes:

"As late as the Middle Ages the witch was still the *hagazussa,* a being that sat on the *Hag,* the fence which passed behind the gardens and separated the village from the wilderness."

Clayton Eshleman writes:

"The hybrid image resonates throughout the Upper Paleolithic .... Such hybrids indicate not only a proto-shamanism but other goals similar to those of countless historical shamanic quests: the recovery of that first unbroken condition when the thoughts & desires of men & women were in fluid & absolute accord with the terrestrial & animal energies surrounding them."

plunge

dive deep-diver

down

down

How does Mermaid figure into the hybridic-shamanic? She

straddles not fence, but Surface. To the extent she engages with

mortals, she participates in the domestic, while poised to spirit to

wild(er)ness with or without an earthly delectable. She smudges

the split between visible & invisible. Thalassa, ocean, is Unfath-

omable, . . . beyond the reach of the rational, — it Excels, . . .

Exceeds,

Mermaid exceeds

She promises promise

how much of

seduction

is promise

the uncharted

the

never-before-experienced

Drawn To

drawn uPon

enchant   muddle   mute

dunked in ambrosial soak

sousing surrep-tition

boiling plasma swirl guttural swash

deep dark sirocco twists

melt

acquiesce

merge

sink

tenebraed to

adjacency

mesh   en-mesh

roil-wrap

partake

pebble babble river rut side rudder sidereal slide

dim, glare-thinning, chasm-collapse

the Fall came early this year

overlap

burnt orange   orange   red   rubescent   russet   risk

                    r   i   c   h

edge-lipping→

vicin-i-ties   (neighborly-ness   — es

grip   inter-lock   /pact impact → tact → tactician

vimineous hive

graft

groan

groan: the heave to exodus

is there an irreverence to chasm? a stain marking the breach?

enterprise: the urge to adjoin

adjoinment: coming together

          commun-i-ty

entrepreneurs are lonely people

abutment, joinery's postulate, implicative snug, . . . fit → fitness

fitness = whole, in-tact, . . . an asunder patch,

rectify // indemnify // swirl →

swirl = adjacency's turbine

concatenate concinnate   //consternate {

                    consternation { = contiguity's blem-

ish

            c   h   u   r   c   h

bells

                 con-gre-gate

in   cin   er   a   t   e

con   struc

t

tenebraed to

old age

creak

crank   y

time's up

ultimatum

disappearance   fade

the turn: you proceed unnoticed, a vanishing, prior selves eclipse,

snuffed by temporal avalanche, no matter the throng, you are ghost,

isolate, a wasting insignificance, an insult, a spur in vitality's hide,

each new sag, each further crease, another condemnation, bodily

defeat, consternation, rebuke, calibrated decline, indiscriminate

ravage, the campaign of no retreat, & to think: it took you by

surprise, as if you couldn't see it coming, despite everything you

know, everything you have witnessed, the biology of decay, but now,

it is you, the insipidity, the arrogance of refuting mortal comeup-

pance, saturated as you are in a culture of denial, a spurious culture

where aging is an embarrassing blemish, which dishes out the

sickly saccharine, which Brands you → over the hill, *Senior Citizen,*

how much of

life

is a

brief-

ing

yet, you are resolute, you think young, lust young, your body is in

collision with your mind, you crave young persons of the opposite

sex *As If* you might hold the least appeal for them, you are

delusional, you are remote & caving, a temporary spasm, a mere

flirtation,

a flesh-slab

tenebraed to

drift

the road to lost road

canopy cutter

detour   dust   indeterminacy

sweep

swirl-swizzle

borealis broth

how much of

the way

is

way-ward

seepage

slope   sideways   slide

       g   l   i   d   e

glisten

glom

gloam

fasten ://: un-fasten

trigger trespass : border invasions

disarray: disarm, distill, , → discharge

re-lease

vent

loam roam lurch riddle

perambulate

flaneur

accrue

in-

gest

tenebraed to

Hinge Theory

lurch	reel	ricochet
rum	in	a
tion		

tenebraed to

trespass

press   pressure   in-dis-pose

bor-der in-vade   toler-ate   stuff your

pockets

usurp   cull   call   collide

collision: drama's meatballs

in the imprecision of wander

tread

tread upon

conquistador   marching orders

trammel

pummel   pulverize   promote   predisposition ://: position

velvet the detour

    . the theorem was lacking practice & sought more control. for a stroll the theorem went for a stroll. there was no place to park.

tenebraed to

seepage   (first mutation)

what gets through   brews   accrues

crewel

— —

a coax c(ur)(oi)ls an alarming

judderbreaks along the seabed

trill rodomontades bisectional hoof

pharoahs clowning

sonorites

sally

tenebraed to

Goat Seep

Arising from "The Hydrogeology of Hudspeth County, Texas."

Permian rock   goat hoof

solidity that bulks, courses, permits, — perusal

porosity: the fraction of total volume occupied by pores or voids

porous/aperture/percolate

sustain

simmer

           brushstroke

cloven hoof rock grasp, — suture/grip groundwater discharge

seepage: accumulating silence

sonority sally & the necessity of ointment

porcelain ://: earth science

how much of

seepage

is

gathering

           [admix clock cochineal

brew, brewing

concocting seepage ghosts

selvage sleuths

from the hurl of hoof pound

where

in the earth is

the

shudder

slither silt slather

stall, impediment, encrustation

circulation bushwhacked

stepping as current, surface flow, dirt fluting

hooves → earth's percussion rim shot baton whisk

voicings

are there conversations between hoof & water, bird & paw,

sediment & moisture?

reciprocal distillations?

communicative troughs?

coruscant envelope bathes

stillness: elegant motion

oneiric fawn

placement ://: pitch ://: pith

unacccountables

tenebraed to

roam

flaneur-waffle

indispose   weighing the

way   jettison   swizzle-surge

                        purl-rustle

                                                            plinth

pacify

         . decide not to decide. but. to incline. to-ward.

seepage-glide-step-gloam

                        , a long way from . . . .

dissoluble

inherency

tenebraed to

wander

f   u   n

frolic

free for all

tumble tendril tentacle rhizome

Libertas

where the buffalo roam

innate / initiate   initial

ize

combust

clearance

tenebraed to

excursion

embark   journey jostle juggle jugular jocular

destination

                              encapsulate: to make fit, provide

here : starting point   to *there*

                here to there

                                    : from/to

near/far

in the interim

                        : interregnum

filigree froth-flounder burble brave knave crave wave

arrival retrieval survival → revival

vitalism

bits blossoms

plum wine

tenebraed to

disarray

uncouth   dismantle   gully

dishevel convolute dissolute derail uninvolve revolve   rev-o-lu-tion

rambunction

relocate

      S was unsullied & conspicuously Neanderthal. to the point of

recidivist peril. no matter. the burn factor.

fringe-flutter → discharge

concourse corrugate   conclude

chaos: a form of dialogue

the lecture circuit: a form of insipidity

offshoot obsidian telepathic rupture

where in the

convergence

is

curriculum

array & the vapors of alliance

tenebraed to

exhume

unearth   exhaust   exhort

e   x   t   r   u   d   e

        intrude

        up-load

divisibility gather cloaca gunnery inevitability probe

anti-gravitational grapple

bring forth   forthright   forti tude   ferocity

diplomacy: rights/privileges/territoriality

prehend : grasp applications & its affect on intimacy

(getting to know, the currency of departures, arriving as an act of

arrangement, disarray: wary & infantilism, 'getting to know you,

know all about ....', circumstantiality & robustness, the capacity to

pause, remote: the far away, — the undisclosed ://: remote device

to control/alter from afar, . . . pithy, treatise, transitional)

f a c e t s : attentiveness ad libs

Pharoah Sanders: Karma, Let's Go Into The House of The Lord

incorporation

the arts of

s e e I n g

tenebraed to

finality

term limits   done   over

term-in-ate

closure   cur   tail   ment

      curtains

   con   clus   ion

   con   clus   ive

aftermath bonfire obsequy the fruits of measurement

frame   border drones   spitfires

inter-loom urgency dispatch

where are you when we need you, Mr. Phillips?

wobbly dustbins the slackers the industrious the human slop

firestorms brimstone blaze patterns bicker save our lord

. when you have gone far & can go no farther you haven't gone far

enough .

adherence

attenuation

discharge

tenebraed to

loafing

sift   soft   supple   *simplicity amulet rills*

                               susurrant swathes

lemonade

goal-punctured

stir-whisk-fulgurate

summer flabby length sunning

grasslands simmer succulence slur

sumptuosity reigns

Zoroaster   slough   slouch

drizz

le

tenebraed to

affability

cordiality   agreeable

the romance of congenial

      chum-worthy

in the temper of amiable this harden, stricken, . . . this crouch

toward afford, final levers lift the nether-posts, . . . recalcitrant ink

spots, plunge scrutinies, . . .

      S wanted to enjoy herself. desperately. unease smote.

gatherings. required. her. to. muster. to put forth. dredge up.

showcase. deliver   .

output.

how much of

output

is

dredge worthy?

worth the moral imperative listen Mr. Higgins when I stop to

consider. whenever. as if there's a trial going on. who? the terms

of the trial are indisposed. is more brutish than outlandish.

qualifications aside the jury reigns. invalidity. judgement. sour.

ing. the vessels are leaky. hard a lee.

cheer   good cheer   cheerfulness

in the daylight of jolly → importunity

ratiocination

tethered to

a

way

out

with

tenebraed

o   v   e   r   c   a   s   t

shadow collapse

accumulate

a summonsing of hives

delectation churns   chives   a

speakeasy elbow

the philosophy of bees

Heraclitus excelled at the 60 yard dash

undertow the claimant the non-obstreperous

current, a livelihood

working

the floor

smelling

tenebraed

Lily   Black Dahlia

   Robin redbreast

confiscated waterways mauled for tribute, bleached

melancholia, patchy lucidities mocked by tide

new mendacities ash the land

punctured tongues lapless

you call me

I call you

eviscerated echoes

scraped

clean

tenebraed to

swarm

smote   disperse

truancy raised to an art form

meander the mandate

as if electric light could trump darkness could

succor soul-crannies with wizened palliatives

acceleration

abandonment

pick-up

tenebraed to a

stretch mathematics (for BK)

fade   wobble-wiggle-wrest   burly-hurly-bounce

numerical flounce   slippery =   woozy isosceles

sighin pi   hectic trigonometric   insufficient coefficient

coddle cuddle cumbersome cooperate   curl trapezius

y^2 = 4ax = spectacular parabola

fit — misfit — bend

airtight delight   congruence, correspondence, — the enormity

of greed

glut, surreption, lachrymose decimal

mete — measure — meddle

numerical cleansing: 'just do the numbers' 'I'm counting on it'

'Mathematically speaking'

numerological *cheer*

massaging/messaging the delight factor

Euclid — Elucidation — Eureka

from gyration this swerve, fissure repair becomes

a form of rebuke,

an indignant hallucination

counting infinity

haze

mystification

tenebraed to

imponderable

lacunae   chasm   undercover

a ghost dance uneasy with tribe courts scofflaw, underbelly, gastric

virulence

spurts of roil-wrath fathom-plunge, rummage-cluster, eke

manifolds, nestle girth   hound   saliva

"For in its highest sense the written numeral is a symbol for what

one can't manage to add up or measure." — Antonin Artaud

      Do you hear Mr. Higgins? Do you sense a turning?

A directional malaise? Scarified indemnities. Pocked mercies.

. addition is nothing more than the admission that nothing adds up

.

turbulence

dread

tenebraed to

petting

affirmation

to   *other*   un

documented   trail blaze

                  outré

voyage from toward

with *in*-fluence

in attendance   attendant   attending to

"The laboratory attendant had raised them [rats] under conditions

in which they were frequently handled, stroked, and had kindly

sounds uttered to them, and they responded with fearlessness,

friendliness, and a complete lack of neuromuscular tension or

irritability." (Montagu)

redolence   songsters thrive best

sufficiently liquidated

touching: treatment, — treat, … trust,

gift, giv-ing   ;   the unspoken garrulous

how much of

petting

is

directional

is impart a departing

return trip plenish flush

illuminate inosculation

pros per i ty

S applied two fingers, then her palm, to her dying mother's fore-

head. S's reaction was varietal: she was sending her mother on her

way; she was peeling part of her self a-*way*.

tenebraed to

attendance

there   here   for   on   upon

     con   front   ing

in the confrontation of manners there

lies a ruse

the comeuppance of querulous   a

spate in the lip of the law

remorse a settled-in set upon

proximity surge   as if in

the lend a lead to

traffic will bear

leisure world

compilations voided

verities spilled

tenebraed to

vacuity

          to

pitted abeyance

stalled conveyor

accumulating wither

to the not that is not

                         (where in the absence is reverb?

Oscillative flaps ashore like an endangered species, vocalisms

deprived of consensus tumble recklessly netted in obliquy, hazard

churls the Scintillative

the disappearance of whistling

hardly matters

tenebraed to

lamentation

lachrymae   equatorial flail   tinder palling at the posts

dearth rags

truckless in Nevada

tenebraed to

lamentation   (first mutation)

ointment-*less*   mould-pound   shudder-stir

desperate for new visions aqueducts taciturn stalled wilt-levers

decondition sobbing in the lobby your place of birth sneer on the

upside the relief is invalid as if in the larynx of proclivity a feint

awaits peculiarity has its own smell

smelling tenebraed in the girth of lamentation (second mutation)

locust swarm   in the dry axe → persuasion, a loot moodi-

ness, a contraband shuffled between nomads

when the ache perpetuates disembarkation's arthritic lid spits a

malevolence cancellable only by foreign exchange, as if in the

larynx of mutiny there lurks *braid,* a twining

as

sembling

tenebraed to

perplexity

plight   riddle   conundrum

    where in the

    query

    is

    drought

the dubious is disinclined to assuage remotely. confrontation

invites evasion. the traps are hardly.

specificity got us here.

tenebraed to

draft

winged transparency   loft assimilative

a current a cast a coating, . . . an uprising

a point of view buffering   a peculiarity bellows

feints   volleys   overtures & puckishness

vroomthistle vom vom

who goes there

tenebraed to

squander

loose change   unravel

    diss   ip   ate

    where in fortitude

    is the

    un-coil

toss reckless diremption wander,   footloose fancy fantail (the stuff of

dreams (so eager on the page)) (to be your suitor, how shall I wear my hair)

pluralistic pastiche

capsize

tenebraed to

gather

reel   reel-in   {ravel}   {revel}

how much

outward

in

reeling-in

scoop bring-to lariat cast longitudinal loosen

the *bring* that fastens → {fascinates

forthwith burgeon , clar i fy

upheavals ruddering threshold shuck invitation bark

climb the tree

tenebraed to

saltatory

soar   spring   fling

    the enterprise of departure

    loss lobs to projection

    vault

how much of

elation is

salta-torial

how much of

bound is

boundless

locomotion from dismissal, leave behind, shed

        nitrogen-rift/respiration-gap

altitudinal shifting

threshold convolution

....s u s t a i n....

dervishing numinous fretboards

compress to

abandon

tenebraed to

tangle

morass   bundlebunglebromide

     huddle

central to the wish is the command the commandment teeter in

the grips of totter Gotterdammerung which is a way of apologizing

for upsurge upcharge reconciliation & revolt

if only you could have been there a slightly step brightly

wish Mr. Philips were alive to see this

hunker down

seraglio

sizzle

by all means call the troops launch a Roman Holiday but beware

the fruit fly

cessation

undetected dormancies

tenebraed to

disparity

lean   inclined   oblique   off center

  unpropitious the terms were settled prior spoke

  wisely without discomfort or beverage

tilt   turn the tables   cessate

grandiloquent tangentiality

the remarkableness of

all fours

tenebraed to

all fours

loco-motion   penumbra   majesty

> "The forward movement of quadrupeds takes place through the
>
> fore and hind limbs with the assistance of the back."

utter   release   sure-ness

> "ears of maple, sails of silk"

baronesses purpling the plain

aeriality spine-combing

                              succulent conversing

how much of step

is

template

          a

direction

          (step in the right direction)

                              {to be a wolf again

                                   on all fours   spine fluid

                                   through the woods

                                {bipedalism the first Fall   our initial

                        remove   remoteness

jostle-spray tier the tired vernaculars

the unfit

chorus-howl ritual chime

pine blossoms   the climb to

ultimate rendition   to

the beyond of bone

paw shack

flexion peel

jawline-loop-lunge

appetite

heritage

tenebraed to

inclination

dispatch   the toward that

tilts   deviation from ...

careen velocity

determinatives filtered through expedience, the stuff of slant,

temperature, & apostate

occupancy: the where of is   wherewithal

                                                   withstand

                                                   withdraw

sumptuosity dressed for carousel

border patrol

ribbons of calculus

outlyer

terrain you seek out

pours of legibility

tenebraed to

vanish

to the architecture of disappearance

wrest-spill   de-

formulation

in the presence of fade

linger

tenebraed to

futility

to

collapse   perishment   syllabic flush

transpire fallows respire

      invalidated transparencies

        corrosive lichen

          evaporative speech

in a world gone vacant "going" rescinds

pertinent necessities appear impertinent

polluted meanders

unavoidable void

tenebraed to

dread (first mutation)

to an aby(smal)ssal precondition

                                                 an

advanced dyspepsia

malaise fiends mutiny landscape meditation, declare

serenity defunct, . . . moribund

despair = dread amplified

bamboozle bombard ragged decompose

despair tumbles despair, . . . despairs of

deportation   the

sledge-lop offal-luffing jackhammer dirge

baleful boondoggle   rank carrion   patchwork blemish

retaliatory puss

trampling pox-fired lesion-fields rummaging the indwell of lost,

→ falsified cleats, fictitious handholds, narcoleptic hierophants . . .

dank umber   molten   bituminous

from melancholia this dread, . . .

sinkage

rupture

raze

* "There lives not one single man who after all is not to some extent in despair."
— Kierkegaard

tenebraed to

desuetude

lull   in u til i ty   idle

dislodge   unbuckledismantleunwindrelease

undulate

lilt

from stutter this saunter ~ . ~ . . . ~..

invaginate vacate   fill-fold lush

swilly swash

subduce

      where in the

      meander

      is

      concupiscence

merrimentburst-dissolve

invigorate

does disentanglement ensnarl dislocation

dislocation: a form of disarmament?

inoperable bellows ruminative

drifts toward equidistance

tenebraed to

disquiet

malodor   disjunct   sus

citate

      r   u   s   t   l   e

                    rustler

                    rouse

rinsing bedlam rind

distemper, ataraxia auctioned,   upheaval

ing

ruckus

per   tur   ba   tion

    : dislodge dismantling harmonies fouled turnstile torpitude

    trudge tanked flanked undermined sour   wrack-

weighted

    flunked

          : :

where in

wherewithal

is

bewitchment

perspiration quilting

tremors

* "In the midst of these intestine Disquiets." Swift, *Gulliver*

Dear Linda,

Just wanted to bring you up to date on recent Hinge Developments (or, "recognitions"). As the Hinge Universe Expands & Complexifies, more & more the applications are referring/resourcing to, & seeking nutrition from, one another. No other source has yet been found to consistently provide so much pertinent material. Case in Point: Currently working on "tenebraed to encroach" & felt it would be wise to check out how "trespass" might enrich the investigation/adventure. So:

In SMELLING MARY:
1. with trespass, p. 113

In FROM STONE THIS RUNNING:
1. "trespass in obdurate credulity", p.191
2. "trespass like lolling liquidity", p. 193
3. "trespass in cumulative bruise", p. 194
4. "border broaching trespass", p. 195
5. "with trespass", p.196

And, of course these applications have valuable "Importations" which have often themselves been applicated. This goes back to the Hinge Import/Export/Mining discussed in beginning of "tenebraed manuscript:"

The behavior then, somewhat reflective of this description of "complexity:"

"Once you've accumulated a sufficient diversity of objects at the higher level, you go through a kind of autocatalytic phase transition — and get an enormous proliferation of things at that level. These proliferating entities then proceed to interact and produce autocatalytic sets at a still higher level. An upward cascade of levels upon levels."

— Heller

tenebraed to

encroach

upon   pounce   wrangle   wrest

inveigh intimate

succor seduce   invoke

inroad

penetrate   insert   in-Sertion

             ass er tion

trespass

in obdurate credulity, → plethora

blood rampart sluice survival soused raw holler-roar

the poured upon the pourer &

the rights of man

a crucibled dialect

a dialectic

omission

tenebraed to

interstice

to where in wherewithal

tide-pleat   burbling diastem

where in the numeral

is

fallout

rupture clause   skiff whack   pause ://: combustible

the interrelation of parts promotes healthy gums

elision   dotted eights   inhale

      per *co* *late*

switchbacks   moody mustangs

the cartography of sullen

tenebraed to

absence

dent   in

dent   to leave out

depart   disappear

the is that is not

the there that never was

hollow

evergreen

interstice

injure

garrulous muffled

the look of an expired langoustine

delaying translucence until

the emerald

is properly groomed

tenebraed to

reverie

fermata   cessate   launch   un

burden   loosed from

trammel-prattle

galimatious-gush

boondoggle

      revere nerve-nimbus suspirous swirl   wing-frigate

      mantis-proxy

      above the human nerve domain

lavender

lip-loll

aeration

Note: The 4th line from the bottom is imported from Will Alexander's book title.

tenebraed to

parting

partition   pardon   apart

fulsomely leaning diameters

                        trench warfare

                        strip mining

                        rift-rive

the cartography of glissade

is there lassitude in *away* with the newly dead, a capacity to

stray back, to return more abundantly, aspatially loaded,

uncircumferenced,

. . . plenitudinous

measure disappears with the gone,

                        fugue evaporative

disjoined — the craft of jointure sullied — unglued

where is the pull in part-ing, the wrench-away, . . . tectonic twitch

           . . . disposition to re-position

                        it broke

                        it fell apart

disassemblage

is the disassembled conflagrative

   the conflagrative migratory

patchwork-blister

                  tenuous ://: tenure

shuttle chute seam peril

how much of

jointure

is

resolve

jointure } ↓ {parting

   the velocious differential

is the joined less vacant than the parted

copious vacate tendril wobble   is absence locatable

                           {where in absence is injure

space   *for:*   remorse   sullen   atrophy

in Rothko's "Black In Deep Red" the parts ensemble, after a

prolonged 'regard,' the colors are *released* of color, the rectilinears

collapse, *peel-away,* swim in contagious magnanimity, a sumptuous

suffuse, — dissolve dehisces   *m   o   o   d*

fundamental utterance

bare

issue

HELLER LEVINSON's books include *Wrack Lariat, from stone this running, Smelling Mary,* and *Toxicity: Poems of the Coconut Vulva.* Levinson's poems and writings have appeared in hundreds of journals and literary outlets around the world. The originator of Hinge Theory, he lives in New York where he studies animal behavior.

TITLES FROM BLACK WIDOW PRESS
TRANSLATION SERIES

A Life of Poems, Poems of a Life
by Anna de Noailles. Translated by Norman R.
Shapiro. Introduction by Catherine Perry.

Approximate Man and Other Writings by Tristan
Tzara. Translated and edited by Mary Ann Caws.

Art Poétique by Guillevic.
Translated by Maureen Smith.

The Big Game by Benjamin Péret.
Translated with an introduction by Marilyn Kallet.

Boris Vian Invents Boris Vian: A Boris Vian Reader.
Edited and translated by Julia Older.

Capital of Pain by Paul Eluard.
Translated by Mary Ann Caws, Patricia Terry, and
Nancy Kline.

Chanson Dada: Selected Poems by Tristan Tzara.
Translated with an introduction and essay by
Lee Harwood.

*Creole Echoes: The Francophone Poetry of Nineteenth-
Century Louisiana.* Translated by Norman R.
Shapiro. Introduction and notes by M. Lynn Weiss.

Earthlight (Clair de Terre) by André Breton.
Translated by Bill Zavatsky and Zack Rogrow.
(New and revised edition.)

*Essential Poems and Writings of Joyce Mansour:
A Bilingual Anthology.* Translated with an
introduction by Serge Gavronsky.

Essential Poems and Prose of Jules Laforgue.
Translated and edited by Patricia Terry.

*Essential Poems and Writings of Robert Desnos:
A Bilingual Anthology.* Edited with an introduction
and essay by Mary Ann Caws.

EyeSeas (Les Ziaux) by Raymond Queneau.
Translated with an introduction by Daniela
Hurezanu and Stephen Kessler.

Fables in a Modern Key by Pierre Coran.
Edited and translated by Norman R. Shapiro. Full-
color illustrations by Olga Pastuchiv.

Forbidden Pleasures: New Selected Poems 1924–1949
by Luis Cernuda. Translated by Stephen Kessler.

Furor and Mystery & Other Writings by René Char.
Edited and translated by Mary Ann Caws and
Nancy Kline.

*The Gentle Genius of Cécile Périn:
Selected Poems (1906–1956).*
Edited and translated by Norman R. Shapiro.

Guarding the Air: Selected Poems of Gunnar Harding.
Translated and edited by Roger Greenwald.

The Inventor of Love & Other Writings
by Gherasim Luca. Translated by Julian & Laura
Semilian. Introduction by Andrei Codrescu. Essay
by Petre Răileanu.

Jules Supervielle: Selected Prose and Poetry.
Translated by Nancy Kline & Patricia Terry.

La Fontaine's Bawdy by Jean de La Fontaine. Trans-
lated with an introduction by Norman R. Shapiro.

Last Love Poems of Paul Eluard.
Translated with an introduction by Marilyn Kallet.

Love, Poetry (L'amour la poésie) by Paul Eluard.
Translated with an essay by Stuart Kendall.

Pierre Reverdy: Poems, Early to Late.
Translated by Mary Ann Caws and Patricia Terry.

Poems of André Breton: A Bilingual Anthology.
Translated with essays by Jean-Pierre Cauvin and
Mary Ann Caws.

Poems of A. O. Barnabooth by Valery Larbaud.
Translated by Ron Padgett and Bill Zavatsky.

Poems of Consummation by Vicente Aleixandre.
Translated by Stephen Kessler.

Préversities: A Jacques Prévert Sampler.
Translated and edited by Norman R. Shapiro.

The Sea and Other Poems by Guillevic.
Translated by Patricia Terry. Introduction by
Monique Chefdor.

To Speak, to Tell You? Poems by Sabine Sicaud.
Translated by Norman R. Shapiro. Introduction
and notes by Odile Ayral-Clause.

MODERN POETRY SERIES

ABC of Translation by Willis Barnstone

An Alchemist with One Eye on Fire
by Clayton Eshleman

An American Unconscious by Mebane Robertson

Anticline by Clayton Eshleman

Archaic Design by Clayton Eshleman

Backscatter: New and Selected Poems by John Olson

Barzakh (Poems 2000–2012) by Pierre Joris

The Caveat Onus by Dave Brinks

City Without People: The Katrina Poems
by Niyi Osundare

Clayton Eshleman/The Essential Poetry: 1960–2015

Concealments and Caprichos by Jerome Rothenberg

Crusader-Woman by Ruxandra Cesereanu.
Translated by Adam J. Sorkin. Introduction by
Andrei Codrescu.

Curdled Skulls: Poems of Bernard Bador. Translated by
Bernard Bador with Clayton Eshleman.

Dada Budapest by John Olson

Disenchanted City (La ville désenchantée)
by Chantal Bizzini. Translated by J. Bradford
Anderson, Darren Jackson, and Marilyn Kallet.

Endure: Poems by Bei Dao.
Translated by Clayton Eshleman and Lucas Klein.

Exile Is My Trade: A Habib Tengour Reader.
Translated by Pierre Joris.

Eye of Witness: A Jerome Rothenberg Reader.
Edited with commentaries by Heriberto Yepez &
Jerome Rothenberg.

Fire Exit by Robert Kelly

Forgiven Submarine
by Ruxandra Cesereanu and Andrei Codrescu

Fractal Song by Jerry W. Ward, Jr.

from stone this running by Heller Levinson

Grindstone of Rapport: A Clayton Eshleman Reader

The Hexagon by Robert Kelly

Larynx Galaxy by John Olson

The Love That Moves Me by Marilyn Kallet

Memory Wing by Bill Lavender

Packing Light: New and Selected Poems
by Marilyn Kallet

tenebraed by Heller Levinson

The Present Tense of the World: Poems 2000–2009
by Amina Saïd. Translated with an introduction by
Marilyn Hacker.

The Price of Experience by Clayton Eshleman

The Secret Brain: Selected Poems 1995–2012
by Dave Brinks

Signal from Draco: New and Selected Poems
by Mebane Robertson

Soraya (Sonnets) by Anis Shivani

Wrack Lariat by Heller Levinson

Forthcoming Modern Poetry Titles

Fables of Town & Country by Pierre Coran.
Translated by Norman R. Shapiro.

Funny Way of Staying Alive by Willis Barnstone

Geometry of Sound by Dave Brinks

Memory by Bernadette Mayer

Penetralia by Clayton Eshleman

LITERARY THEORY / BIOGRAPHY SERIES

*Barbaric Vast & Wild: A Gathering of Outside and
Subterranean Poetry (Poems for the Millennium, v5).*
Jerome Rothenberg & John Bloomberg-Rissman

Clayton Eshleman: The Whole Art by Stuart Kendall

Revolution of the Mind: The Life of André Breton
by Mark Polizzotti

WWW.BLACKWIDOWPRESS.COM